JENNIFER BROWNE

AMERICAN CROW

JENNIFER BROWNE

AMERICAN CROW

www.beltwayeditions.com

Printed in the United States of America
10 9 8 7 6 5 4 3 2 1

Book Design: Jorge Ureta Sandoval
Cover photograph: Quinton Browne.
Author Photo: Jennifer Browne
ISBN: 978-1-957372-13-6

Beltway Editions (www.beltwayeditions.com)
4810 Mercury Drive
Rockville, MD 20853
Indran Amirthanayagam: Publisher
Sara Cahill Marron: Publisher

Contents

Triage

Reliquary of My Hands

Loving the Broken

The Steep Decline

What We Pass Down

Witness

****

TRIAGE

****

Maeve's Grave

In County Sligo, I climb Knocknarea to reach the passage tomb of Maeve, warrior queen of Irish myth, killed with a piece of hard cheese. The stone path is deeper than the surrounding fields, "worn down by the traffic of ages," as Robert Macfarlane describes these holloways. This feels more like a hallowed-way—a sunken path hollowed by the feet of pilgrims.

At least it has been. Visitors now clamber over Maeve's cairn, dislodge stones. A haphazard foot might finally permit archaeology, might prove Maeve is there, buried upright, armed for battle, facing her enemies in Ulster.

The point is, of course, not if she is but that she might be. People seek the cairn not with the surety that it is empty, but in the belief that it is full.

The Mole Crab

Finding the armored bodies of sand crabs under our tide-washed feet at Assateague, my aunt tells me they are a delicacy in Peru, where she lives. This is my first hint that things are moving beneath us, the world awash in protein.

The Peripheral

The term *sonder* was created for the online *Dictionary of Obscure Sorrows* to indicate "the realization that each random passerby is living a life as vivid and complex as your own." In films, a character might gaze across a city at office buildings dotted with lights, other people working late.

A passenger, I look out of the car window, know the trees along the road, the rocks, the leaf litter are rich in critters: deer, raccoons, snakes, and opossums, their waddling bellies fat with ticks.

Bears

A guide to spotting winter dens recommends ruffling a dampened hand through the leaf litter of a suspected den to check for bits of dark fur. I swab the floors of rock crevices and behind the roots of a fallen tree and find only my own muddied palm.

Later, driving, I recall a naturalist's report that black bears sometimes hibernate in highway culverts. I scan the hillsides, don't see bears. I can't even see the culverts.

Outcroppings at Antietam

The path to Maeve's grave reminds me of the sunken road at Antietam. Farm lane-turned-earthwork, it sank before its pilgrims started walking it. From the sunken road, one might see the surrounding fields as a smoothed blanket, might miss the small eruptions of limestone and dolomite that dot the landscape. Soldiers sought shelter under these outcroppings, brief shields lean as the men themselves. An amateur historian tells me they are mapped on geologic surveys, these shelters, but in reading about the rock formations, I find only notes on the general karst landscape. Information, too, is eroded away.

Binary

The Lepidodendron scale fossils embedded in the sandstone along the water's edge appear to be machined. I stepped over them for years thinking the pattern unnatural. Even now, knowing what they are, it seems unlikely.

The kayak cuts the duckweed, leaves a path along the surface like an otter might. How few other tracks I leave—no breaks in undergrowth, no scat. The road and sidewalks unmarked by my steps. The mud unsmeared. My most observable traces are digital, accumulating drifts of data I don't understand in places I'll never see.

Relativity

In an aside to his presentation at Ellwood Manor, the docent laments that layering periods of history confuses visitors, that he can only say Grant's headquarters were nearby, not that the Marquis de Lafayette also walked this land, his troops bound for Yorktown. The docent is spry and scales the carved front steps of the house quickly, but I guess he's in his mid 70s, nearly the number of years that separated Grant and Lafayette.

In any one place, how many layers of history can we keep track of? Does one thread always lift to the surface?

Arm of Stonewall Jackson / May 3 1863

I have driven for more than three hours to see the burial place of Stonewall Jackson's arm.

I could say that I have made this trip to make the idea of loss comprehensible, that the sheer number of Civil War casualties can't be understood without focusing on a single story, but I'm here because I've recently scattered a friend's ashes. The calcified granules of his remaining body clung to my pants hem, to the plastic bag in the urn. Having left him spread so thinly, I feel I need to see a grave.

This one strikes me as a kindness. A chaplain plucked the discarded arm from a pile of amputated limbs, placed it into the wooden box that would become its coffin, and carried it to a family cemetery for Christian burial. It may not matter that it was disinterred, that this may not be where it was reburied, that it may have never been Jackson's arm at all. Perhaps the arm, at last, needs to be a surrogate for the other limbs on the pile, the tree-shaded stone marker a reminder of the unmarked limb-pits that must be nearby.

Leaving there, I drive home through what I know have been landscapes of suffering, but I sing along to radio songs, realize I've now been to Jackson's arm's grave precisely as many times as I have been to my father's.

The Rabbits

Chore-weeding in my parents' garden, I accidentally uncover a nest of baby rabbits, their bodies fitted together like gears. Thoughtless, I pluck one from the cluster, hold its timid body next to my heart. My brother warns me away from touching the others, says the mother rabbit will starve them all because this one smells of human.

With that, I learn the horror of desire, of mercy.

But it's a myth. The mother will come back to a re-covered nest, will accept a child's hands on her own child. Nearly forty years later, I don't know if I have only imagined the bunnies abandoned, if I never saw them dead in the fur-lined nest.

The rabbits in my garden are eastern cottontails. Unsociable, they live alone, cleanly demarcating their territory. That they would take back the child-smudged bunny seems both automatic and generous. I can't decide which version I prefer.

People assume a nest has been abandoned only because the mother isn't visible. I would say we don't make that assumption about humans, but we do. Of the children wandering along the dual-lane highway, I think, where is their mother? Where was my own mother when I discovered the rabbits? Why don't I ask about the fathers?

Tracks

In its burrowing, a groundhog displaces and discards a human jawbone from a New York soldier, one of the Antietam dead. In the intervening years, how many people have walked over that spot, how many animals? What was uncovered by the soldiers who bivouacked overnight, tense before the fog on the morning of the battle; what was later uncovered by the farmers whose land was salted with blood?

At Antietam, the land is hallowed, but I think of the bones as being elsewhere—taken back to their families or interred in the national cemetery in Sharpsburg.

Across the Atlantic, Maeve's pilgrims walk to see a grave that may not contain her. The land on which I roved to get to Knocknarea was also sacred, beset with shallow foundation traces of houses fallen in on themselves, houses where the last task of the last of the family was to close and lock the door on his own famine-death, sparing the passersby.

Without an historical marker, the land is just a sheep graze.

The soldier's bone shards were buried at Saratoga. There are still too many men listed as missing-in-action among the twenty-four New York units that fought near the Cornfield for his grave to be marked with a name.

Lessons From the Pry House

Supposedly Mel Brooks said "Tragedy is when I cut my finger. Comedy is when you fall into an open sewer and die." Antietam is a place where I am reminded that whatever it is I feel to be tragedy is, ultimately, a cut on my finger.

During the battle of Antietam, Dr. Jonathan Letterman used the Pry property as headquarters for the Medical Department. Letterman devised the ambulances for treating and evacuating casualties from the battlefield. His system included the application of triage.

What am I doing at Antietam, at Ellwood, at Sligo but triage for a *something*, a wound that I can't see?

The Visitors' Center

Emptiness is an opportunity, a mystery. A child lifts the log-lid from the resin habitat diorama in the state park visitors' center to reveal the coiled copperhead. Afterward, every hollow log promises a flash of danger.

The Priest's Cave

The limestone band that connects Sligo and Antietam is porous. It opens into holes, is carried away in solution, washed with the carbonic acid of carrion, of decay. These are spaces for bats, for liverwort, for bootleggers, hermits, for vows of silences. Ducking out of a storm, I stand in an echoing amphitheater. The wind passes through the lean spaces, becomes musical. Everything about this cave seems holy, and each breath I take here, each fiber of lint that whiskers from me onto the walls continues its ruining.

Finding Bones

I am sent to the field guide by a hawk picked clean by carrion beetles. Hollows in the bones allow for flight, of course, but the cross-section illustration calls to mind not soaring, but savoring: a riddled loaf of ciabatta. To hold a rustic loaf is to invoke earlier bakers, the biga calling wild yeast out of the air. The hawk's skull sits on a shelf, silent.

Bowerbird

The male satin bowerbird is well-known for building a
courtship "arena," placing sticks and objects as blue as
his eyes to entice a willing female. After his strutting and
prancing, his tiling of baubles, after the mating, the female
is left to build her own nest, to hatch the young alone.

Nests

Through the semester, I watched a songbird build a precarious nest in a thin tree, held my breath while walking by, even amid storms, lest I be the one to dislodge it. I am arrested by nests. The oriole's pendulous pouch, the osprey's platform, the grackle's softened bowl. Each a marvel.

I've made my own precarious nests, built body-spaces for the nurtured: the breast hollow into which I've fitted curves of cheeks, the uterine nest lined with blood, itself a winter den abandoned. Most nights, now, the cat finds her safe depression in the flattened space behind my curled knees. She sleeps, trapping me.

Of Unseen Hollows

An illusion of solidness, I press against surfaces and feel my own weight, resistance, but I am filled with hollows, gaps for cerebrospinal fluid, parasites, blooming microflora.

Skeletal calcium wears down, over centuries becomes an element of limestone, which itself wears down. The body in the ground becomes the ground. The bones of feet become components of the stones on which we walk.

The meadow that appears as a blanket of green is, closer, inlaid with rabbit tracks. The soil is granular. The rabbit, cleaned for cooking, gleams under the knife.

****

RELIQUARY OF MY HANDS

****

Life Drawing

I earned beer and cigarette money in college by sitting as a model for a life drawing club. It was twice the fee for nude models, but embarrassed by the pale dough of my belly, I was always clothed.

Years later, one of the artists recognizes me, describes in detail the buffet of my body, my frank nakedness couched in the clean light.

He still has the drawings, he says.

Remembrancer

"Using photographs as an instrument
of memory is probably a mistake because
I think that photographs actually sort
of impoverish your memory in certain ways,
sort of take away all the other senses
—the sense of smell and taste and texture,
that kind of stuff."

Sally Mann

Can the attentive use a photograph to propel senses? Can they use the photograph as a lover's eye—to absorb each plane of a face, each dappled flash in an iris, each mole and hair and textured patch on the beloved's body?

What if the body of my beloved is a salt marsh, a vernal pool?

A friend claims that choosing not to photograph forces our attention to the moment, to see it instead of the framing viewfinder, but without scrolling through these images, can I remember where I was on Wednesday of last week?

The Lover's Eye

I've thought that if I were blindfolded in a dark room with a congregation of naked men I could pick out a body I love by touch alone. It's not just the appeal of quantity, or the singularity of my beloved, but the belief that my attention was so careful, so aware, I'd know his body better than any other, even better than my hand.

I've forgotten the last name of the first man about whom I thought this.

Another Redheaded Model

While sitting, I'd foreshorten my pose or complicate my hands, make myself a challenging subject.

Sometimes, though, I'd embody the models whose shapes I knew in my bones. All the *stunners* of the Pre-Raphaelites, Klimt's gilt serpents, the pale arms of Munch's "Vampire."

And always at the periphery, the red winter wheat of Helga's braids.

In an interview, Testorf said she was "reborn" when Wyeth first painted her, that "Somebody was really looking at [her]—really seeing [her]."

I looked for that in the eyes behind the easels, but at their best, I walked away from those sessions feeling like a plate of shimmering oysters, a dead pheasant.

Albums

We don’t have them anymore.

My mother piled her mixed-decade photos into boxes, unlabeled, uncurated. I identify some family members and take guesses elsewise.

Mine are Hast cheekbones, and I scan the box of photos for that same face, feel a community of ancestors, only some with shared blood.

Hidden Mother

In some 19th C. photographs, women draped in fabric steadied squirming toddlers for the long exposure, blending into the background like furniture, draperies. The point, of course, to have an image of this child in a time of death-in-childhood, a treasure in case of diphtheria, TB, ill-tempered fathers.

I think of these mothers, their still-visible shapes, their spectral hands, when I look at the wealth of photos of my child, think of them when I notice my own invisibility in images, in the daily spaces into which I disappear.

"All the valley's hushed"

"[N]egative events tend to be remembered in a more accurate fashion than positive events."

Elizabeth Kensinger

What I remember of my father's funeral is speaking—
telling my drunk uncle to leave. He complied: my heavy-
pregnant body a cause for fear.

What I remember of my child's birth was silence,
burrowing in beyond language.

Why have I admired my mother's reserve? Why do I
admire my own? The deepest emotions of my life have
been silent, rendered incapable of speech by fear or love or
wonder.

Though I saw the easy weep as weakness, I regret, now,
that closed self, wish I had been more kind as my uncle left
my mother's house singing "Danny Boy."

How much of this do I really know; how much do I trust?
Isn't there something to be said for building the story I
need over time?

Talisman

From a wide wedding band, my mother had a sculptural ring made, a gift I never wore. My Great-Aunt Cassie's ring, she said. I sold it when the ounce price rose. But in a jewelry box I have another wide wedding band, which I name as Cassie's.

They can't both have been hers; she only married once. In my childhood, that marriage was held up as happy, the proof their close deaths. "Whither thou goest, I will go," even into the vast nothing. It's only recently that, stripped of the bedtime story, I've thought about the happenstance of death, that no one ever romanticized the one who died first.

Still, I've made totems of other things, purchased objects like those owned by people I loved. Same-patterned plates, decoys made by other carvers. They needed only to be held against the idea of a person, made holy by the reliquary of my own hands.

French Postcards

In the Photo Antiquities museum, I'm transfixed by a lit display of stereoscopic negatives. In one, nearly-twin views of a woman with a lifted hem, a loop and button garter strap pressing into her thigh. I can imagine how her knees would seem to come forward in the three dimensions of the stereoscope, can feel the desire of everyone who has looked at her looking back at them from this tin-framed peepshow window. I blush with remembered sense memories: a desired, desiring face framed by my own knees.

I think of a different museum, on exhibit an ancient oil lamp that, lit, would have set to movement the embossed lovers before the flame.

I'd like a little more art, more artifice, but now it's a wealth of texted penises: unclean-bathroom selfies of dicks with their cocks out.

Washtub

In my desk is a photo of my father and his younger sister in a metal washtub. It's probably 1944. He's smiling, standing in loose undershorts, holding an unshucked ear of corn. They are healthy, rounded American children.

My father is dead. My aunt is in Peru. Even if I could ask them about this photo, what could they tell me? Given the corn, it may have been taken in West Virginia at their grandparents' farm, but it could have been in Maryland, their parents' garden plot.

Does it matter where they were, why they needed washing?

I name my father's expression *mischievous*, an interpretation. Before his death, I was estranged from him, but the stories I heard at his funeral, the ones I most like—most want to be like—reflect playfulness.

What are the photographs of which I'm fond? They're all of other people.

Of Estrangement

I was estranged from my father. I doubt he knew he was estranged from me.

Helga

The poet remarks, sitting in the winter light, on my resemblance to Wyeth's Helga.

This is a compliment for which I've waited decades, having seen myself in her grey-brown turtleneck, her green coat, her naked, waking stretch. I'm startled to feel seen in this man's seeing another man's visions of another woman, some of which were painted the year I was born.

Although I want to know which part of which painting he's seeing, my pale throat flushes with shame, vanity. I don't ask.

****

LOVING THE BROKEN

****

Of The Sorrows

I don't know where I first read the story of Deirdre of the Sorrows, but I was young enough to have forgotten—or not understood—the role of Conchobar, claiming and raising the beautiful, cursed infant in claustration.

What I remembered was Deirdre's seeing the blood of the slaughtered pig, the snow, the black wings of the raven, its beak tearing at discarded scraps. And I remembered her longing, her desire for those colors on a face she'd yet to see.

Like all long-told stories, this one is shifty. Sometimes it's a calf cut open, or dead-as-prey lamb in the wood. Sometimes the raven sips the blood congealing on the surface of the snow.

The consistent bit is a beautiful girl's learning from a dead thing what arouses her—then all hell breaking loose.

Reeds

Chihuly's red glass reeds were installed in an outdoor reflecting pond, visible through the glass wall of the museum. Ice had slid from the roof, breaking the reeds to shards on the snow.

Where Deirdre fell in love with the color of the blood, looked for that red on the lips of Naoise, I think I fall in love with the brokenness, the valuable thing placed intentionally where it will be destroyed. On how many lips have I looked for--and found--that?

Family Laniidae

“derived from the Latin word for ‘butcher’”

A man to whom I’m attracted shares a poem about green jays, and in it I want to hear myself.

The field guide already on the table, I spend the rest of the day on jays—bright corvids with long memories, pair bonded for life.

Earlier, I read about a shrike’s using the barb of a barbed-wire fence to impale a grasshopper. The same recognizably human intelligence—using tools to destroy, to sustain.

Maybe it’s the shrike in which I should hear myself—
trilling with a clear song while I find other hands to be
sharp for me, to be lethal.

Blood on the Lip

On the list of services of a local salon is something called *vampire*,"a simple in-office procedure using Platelet Rich Plasma to enhance the fullness of women's anatomy, specifically the labia majora." I think of Elizabeth Bathory, who purportedly bathed in the blood of virgins to preserve her youth and beauty. Contemporary paintings show her to be dark haired with a little Hungarian sadness in her green eyes.

However she is "infamously remembered," her gory baths become less and less likely as scholars uncover truths—her wealth, the debts owed to her cancelled upon her imprisonment, the evidence written after her death.

And though my own labia are still regularly reddened, rinsed with admittedly non-virginal platelets, they persist in being visibly middle-aged. There's no magic to it: the blood in which I'm washed is a clearing of a nest, not a potion of despoiled and vibrant life.

I shudder to think of all those beautiful young women who have been punished for blood someone else thought was a child.

Courtship

A cluster of males circles a lone female. She flits about; they land nearby, preening, calling, chattering their *"jay, jay"* call, their *"queedle-queedle."* She flits; they whirl. It repeats. Eventually, one by one, all the males fall away but one, who becomes her mate-for-life.

The wild bird food company describes an individual male's quitting the pursuit as "a self-selecting process where he decides his interest can't outrun the other birds."

At first I want to issue a lament for the female, her lack of agency, her being left. I've felt that outstripped interest, fear it. But I've chased, too, can think of times when it was best, weary and panting, to just wave someone else along.

An Uncomfortable Truth

I'm a squanderer at heart.

Trailing me is a wide wake of abandoned, precious things:
a waiter presents a menu, and the last meal's perfect bite
turns to ash.

Never a Dead Thing

I'll revise: Deirdre didn't learn her desire from a dead thing. What bled on the snow before her clear or weeping eyes (here, again, the shifting story) was labor to sustain through the long winter, a hollowed body with human-like skin.

When we look at any meal, do we see the sacrifice? Do we see the animal in the meat? The fields of grain leading forward this flesh? Can we see anything of what shape it will take in us?

What Deirdre saw in that fresh-butchered body was the face of Naoise, her realized love, the blasted future against which she wagered herself.

Of the Sorrows II

Though Deirdre's known by the sorrows she's caused, like
Helen, she didn't. The "terrible evil" that came from her
was Conchobar's pride, his raw wanting.

Her only choices were to love Naoise, to grieve unsleeping
and unsmiling for a year, to cast herself upon the rock
that split her lovely head. Those sorrows are the story's
forgotten or disregarded appendices.

American Crow

I’m a crow finding what's shiny and presenting it, token, to one who has shown me kindness, that these beak-clasped gifts might shift their notice from what’s sharp at my mouth.

But now I’ve read a crow’s beak isn’t sharp enough, or hard, to pierce carrion skin.

Else they'd starve, crows follow something else’s breaking open, and maybe I've had it wrong. Maybe it’s no gift, but an empty beak eating at the places where others have done the work, the weakening.

First-Born Son

I tell the visiting poet I'm anxious about my son's leaving home. He asks if my son is an only child, and when I say he is, the poet responds, "and he's your son." There's such tender emphasis on that word son, such cultural weight in his voice. But my son was born a daughter and, magicked, is becoming this truer self.

Until I heard son in a mouth that valued the maleness, the powerful patrilineality of it, I hadn't heard the unspoken prophesies of my child's birth, hadn't reckoned the prophesies to which he's now laid claim.

Another Beautiful Child

For years, taped to the interior of my desk was a photograph: a rosie-ring of Romanian orphans, the image blurred by the photographer's or the children's movement. I can still call to mind the shining face at the lower right turned toward the camera, her cloudy-cataracted eyes reflecting an unseen sky.

The terms used by the American Academy of Ophthalmology to categorize pediatric cataracts or "opacities"—*progressive blue dot, cerulean, lenticular*—raise warm associations and then raise a reprimand that these—Voyager's photo of Earth, a vase shaped like cupped leaves, a horse trotting a raspy panel—are all things I know how to see, have seen. These terms came from the mouths of sighted doctors.

But why did I keep this photograph, X-actoing it from a magazine? The child's raised and moonlike face? Her moonstone eyes? The movement of play? My wanting to bring her into my life even if I couldn't bring her out of the orphanage?

I wanted to keep her, but only in this one unreconciled and glowing view, which I kept cloistered behind the escritoire's hinged panel.

****

THE STEEP DECLINE

****

Inheritance

The National Institute on Alcohol Abuse and Alcoholism reports a nearly even split between genetic and environmental factors in determining whether someone will become an alcoholic.

Every drinker I know comes from a family of drinkers.
Every family I know is a family of drinkers.

Another Central Appalachian Town

This is a small early-nineteenth century town founded on coal and transportation, a stagecoach stop that grew. It's now a college town, and the university is its heart, its primary employer. And three call centers. There are fifteen churches. Twelve bars. Two liquor stores. One looking for company will find it in a bar on any weeknight, a church on Sunday morning.

Recognition

Walking, I pass college rentals, their sidewalks piled with trash bags filled with pizza boxes, convenience food, empty bottles of beer. Case boxes form a bulwark around one porch. The first business I pass is a liquor store, a former grocery now stocked with booze, snacks, thinning onions. They open at 9:00. Sometimes a person stands outside, waiting, edgy. We nod at each other.

Disturbing Film Night

Two friends and I used to entertain ourselves with what we called Disturbing Film Night. We'd pick films, make themed dinners to match. One of us—Kurt—insisted on a drink to go with the dinner, the film. He's now dead: a slow death, intentional with alcohol. I tried to keep him alive through trips to the hospital, roasted chickens, and, later, bottles of Ensure, which became all he could stomach. The other follows suit. If I see him, my first question is whether he is eating. I know he has largely stopped; what money he has goes to bottles of Zelko.

Any Taco Tuesday

My student intern tells me about her family history; her
mother warned her about drinking in college. She has become
the designated driver, describes her "drunk girl" friends
as being like "funny toddlers" singing karaoke after heavy
margaritas at the Mexican place in a neighboring town. A
glow falls over the image as she tells it, but I ask about the
people in the next booth. A family with two small children.

Derby Day

On the fourth of July, we celebrate our independence with a soapbox derby on the steep decline that is Main Street. Children under twelve race the cars, try to not crash into hay bales that line the route. It's one day of the year when the city suspends its open container ban, and crowds come out to cheer the racers, drink canned beer in the sun. For a few years, the organizers tried to ban alcohol. Attendance fell too low; even the sno-cone sales were down.

Lazarus

The addiction we hear about now is opiate, not alcohol. Halfway through the year, 26 people had died in my small county from overdose. Others have been called back to life by Naloxone, which the health department trains addicts' families to carry. Holding the atomizer must be both consoling and terrifying. Any event of survival is another opportunity for death.

Otis

An internet search of TV shows with alcoholic characters
does not return *The Andy Griffith Show.*
My childhood's stuffed bear, nose askew, was named
Otis after Hal Smith's lovable town drunk. What does
this say about what comforts me? What is clear is that
the alcoholic on our screens is largely comedic: one eye
squinty, his talk strange, too truthful. But an alcoholic is
only comedic for those who can change the channel.

Revisionist History

Too many times, I've tried to write myself out of other people's memories of my drinking—e-mails sent out the morning following a bender: "X., Forgive me for my revelry, my overt affection, my ill-considered language. I enjoyed spending time with you." The subtext is that I know—but can't really remember—I was a mess; I awoke in a rush of glucose and self loathing from metabolizing booze.

Charisma

Until you're sloppy or broke, everyone loves you in bars. They're good for a hard luck story until it goes on too long. After that happens, the food pantries and the AA meetings are in the churches. They love you at the meetings, too, but that love is more demanding, asks for more than a round.

Drinking to Forget

He did.

I thought alcohol was a solvent, washing bits of memory, but booze keeps new memories from setting. Those times, those places where we were never stuck.

It's almost sadder than thinking of them washed away. If he lost the memory, there was a thing for which to grieve, a hope for recovery, but if it never formed, it was nothing.

What should I think about what he said he felt?

Revisionist History II

Tourists come to these mountains to see early American history, the French and Indian War and the C&O Canal, the B&O Railroad. In the summer, the local museum commemorates the Whiskey Rebellion. Wavery from white whiskey tastings, I pose with life-sized cut-outs of Washington and Hamilton, national heroes whom we might, at this celebration, regard as enemies of the cause.

There was a time when whiskey kept us afloat, when it was safer to drink than water.

Weights

Norm, my great uncle, was a bootlegger. He could make anything work, could pick up garage detritus and build something useful: a tuna can became a flashlight I keep tucked in a drawer.

He went by the nickname Cheese because his Uncle Toady, a grocer, paid him to sell salty cheese in bars. He—and the bartenders—sold more of their wares, kept the men drinking longer. Only now do I think about what that meant for the women to whom they went home.

Norm drank Crown Royal whisky, stored antique paperweights in the flannel bags. My first memory of alcohol has to do with those treasures, my longing to hold those palm-round, shimmering worlds.

Processing

"Alcohol is metabolized by several processes or pathways. The most common of these…involves two enzymes—alcohol dehydrogenase (ADH) and aldehyde dehydrogenase (ALDH). These enzymes help break apart the alcohol molecule…First, ADH metabolizes alcohol to acetaldehyde…Then, in a second step, acetaldehyde is further metabolized down to another, less active byproduct called acetate."

National Institute on Alcohol Abuse and Alcoholism

This is what I know. The metabolism of one prodigious drinker smells the same as any other. It is immediate, visceral. One of my students appears to be practicing the life of a drinker in the way one practices monasticism.

In my office, I see her only through a wave of panic.

Jesus in the Sheetz

Waiting to pay for my coffee, I exchanged a greeting with a man standing by the windows. He said he was trying to get to the next town, where his girlfriend would wire him money, and he could catch a bus to Ohio.

I walked out and back in, offered him a lift. Jittery in the passenger seat, he tells me about his having been in jail, talks about his girlfriend, how he's slowly learning to be the kind of man she should be with.

While driving, I think about my atheism, my lack of faith, but if there were such a walking being as Jesus, he would need a ride, would smell like wine, would talk about approaching the world with love.

No Way to Revise this History

The other Disturbing Film Night friend died alone in Pennsylvania, the distances between us greater than geography. I haven't been to his grave. I don't know where his grave is.

I memorialize him alone, soberly.

Do You See What I See?

I've been present for two detox hallucinations. Each time, the hallucinator trusted his vision, but I could not trust it or my own, that there weren't tiny animals cavorting under the chair, that there wasn't a dreadlocked baby in the room.

Having seen another person's certainty in an hallucination, I've come to question my own certainties, to feel fear when my belief becomes too strong.

Rock Bottom

Before he died, while he was still only losing track of days and vomiting blood, Kurt's sister called, questioned my hope.

Her warning: "There is no rock bottom. Rock bottom is death."

My idea of hitting bottom had been like swimming down to the floor of a deep pool. To descend, lungs stinging, and scrape against the rough tile is to be reassured a sturdy something contains what suspends you.

There is no ladder at the edge.

****

WHAT WE PASS DOWN

****

Black-Capped Chickadee

A database of bird sightings at Finzel Swamp shows the black-capped chickadee as common throughout the year. The Peterson Guide says the chickadee's voice is a "clearly enunciated *chick-a-dee-dee-dee or dee-dee-dee.*" It's song "a clear whistle, f*ee-bee-ee or fee-bee*, first note higher."

It is a fault of my listening, not my hearing, that I still only know the chickadee by sight.

What We Want to See

"In the last analysis, it is human consciousness which is the subject matter of history. The interrelations, confusions, and infections of human consciousness are, for history, reality itself."

Marc Bloch

Maybe any human study is about human consciousness. The observer not only influences the observed, but constructs it.

We think of nurturing families, of courtship among the pairs of animals we see, wax rhapsodic about their tenderness, forgetting the enclosure, the house, the terrain break keeping them with each other.

We've been told all birds mate for life, but researchers paternity-testing chicks say not all parents are monogamous.

As this flock of chickadees breaks into pairs, I know some partnered females will also seek out higher-status males from among the community. These selective infidelities just a temporary stepping out, a breeding strategy.

Some of the hatchlings will be more successful, but it doesn't teach any of the lessons about love I might have hoped to learn.

Viewing Finzel from Albuquerque

At a wilderness conference, a presenter suggests satellite photos and virtual tours could keep people from *trammeling* the land, could provide access or give meaning to wilderness spaces for those who couldn't—or wouldn't—travel to them.

Homesick in the hotel room, I look at the swamp via Google Earth, trace the trail with my cursor.

Imagine the thousand data points—the bunched and widened topographical lines, the species survey list, rhythmic audio files, even the grid of a high-res image—of the surface of the face of one whom you love. How pale is that data in contrast to what it denotes?

I want to say there is no parcel of land I know as well as Finzel, yet I've been lost there, panicked and disoriented. In truth, the parcel I know is barely the swath of the path. I still can't name the plants, forget to call the salamanders *newts*.

Sainte-Terrer

John Muir disapproves: "I don't like either the word or the thing. People ought to saunter in the mountains - not hike!" Muir appropriates Thoreau's etymology for saunter: "'from idle people who roved about…and asked charity, under pretense of going…to the Holy Land, till the children exclaimed, 'There goes a Sainte-Terrer,' a Saunterer, a Holy-Lander."

They both present the land itself as holy, those who walk into it as pilgrims, but Thoreau calls "every walk…a sort of crusade…to go forth and reconquer this Holy Land from the hands of the Infidels."

At any given time, who are the infidels? Whose sacred is more holy?

The features of the path—the fenceposts, foundations, gravestones, farm pond—were left by generations of infidels. So, too, the beavers, dogs, the hunters, the girls who come to swim and leave stubbed-out, smoked-down butts beside the summer-grass indentations of their bodies.

Contemporary etymologists say Thoreau was probably wrong: *saunter* is more likely from the Middle English *santren*, to muse, or from the French *s'aventurer*, to venture.

As for my own sauntering, perhaps a more fitting root is the earlier *swantrelle*, pretender.

Quarry

At speed, a Merlin snatches a songbird out of the air, drops, lands on a fencepost. It's an elegant bird, slaty and sleek. I learn later, leisurely with the field guide, that Merlins were once called *lady hawks*, used by noblewomen to hunt skylarks.

Earlier in the year, I watched an austringer and his hawk hunt shrews on a castle's grounds, admired the tensing talons on the leather glove, the patience of the training. I ignored the tether.

On the fencepost, the Merlin tugs at strips of viscera, bloodies its beak. The tall grass is snowy with down.

First-Day Hike

Nothing out but a black-capped chickadee, precarious and sideways on a seedy branch. The deer have left spoor, but they keep hidden in the thickets.

At the hollowed base of a tree, a path of blurred tracks through the snow, tiny feet seeking shelter.

I'm grateful to see only four-legged tracks; I have made the mistake of, again, forgetting hunting season doesn't necessarily end.

St. Patrick Departs Appalachia

I had been going to the swamp for twenty years before I saw a snake there. The first was a black snake, shocking in its length, then a racing-striped ribbon snake, and garter snakes, their checkerboard backs like zippers. Each caused a start, a shudder.

Depending whom you ask, Patrick slew the last of the great serpents of Ireland at Lough Derg, which takes its name—the red lake—from the serpent's blood. My Catholic mother's own inclination, too, is to raise a shovel, to slay.

It was only after I started to see the water snakes that I sought them out, realized I had lost the snake-sight cringe, forgot the dainty, crushing foot of Mary on the serpent's head.

The field guide names the northern water snake an aggressive species, yet they stayed still, entwined, a caduceus.

Snakes can teach us observation or change-through-growth, our old skins, old selves, splitting and falling away. The eyes of a snake about to molt turn milky Mary-blue, are nearly blind. I want to hope growth follows after a necessary lack of vision.

Cultivar

Eleven years before the great famine, before blight blackened the fields of Irish lumpers, Joseph Paxton planted a banana for the Duke of Devonshire in the grand conservatory of Chatsworth House.

This banana, the Cavendish, was later crated and carried by missionaries. It filled the fields of plantations, multiplied like Christianity, became a different, edible body, its sturdy skin unblemished.

It supplanted the Gros Michael, which had, itself, spread with colonialism outward from a botanist's specimen in Martinique, driving economies, binding labor, and was then decimated commercially, leaving a shade of itself for us to taste in isoamyl acetate, in the yellow stretch of banana Laffy Taffy.

It was the Gros Michael in the hands of *Curious George*, and now the stacks of hands at the grocery are more linked to monkeys than missionaries, estates, laborers, plantations, boats and republics. Martinique is still French. Chatsworth House is open for tours, and the current Duke of Devonshire sued the Republic of Ireland over his claim of rights to wild salmon.

The skeletal limbs of the famine memorial at Murrisk arc, a coffin ship of bodies, a warning about monoculture, colonized powerlessness. Across the corpse-dense Atlantic, clones of Paxton's Cavendish splotch toward brown on my counter.

Genealogy

In the photograph, I am a blanket-bundled, bored child sitting on the table of a grave. To my right is my uncle, making a charcoal rubbing of the stone.

I haven't seen this photograph in years. I don't remember the name of the ancestor on whom I sat, only now consider how disrespectful I was, having been taught to avoid stepping the body-length below a headstone.

Does the photograph work similarly to the search for the ancestor? I've documented it in relation to myself. Glancing through branches of generations, considering, even, sending away a vial of DNA-rich spit, isn't my concern about what these people, whose lineages and legacies I carry bodily, tell me about myself?

Although my uncle has traced us into the 16th century, most folk remember only two generations. Otherwise, it's stories, my great-grandmother's thick braid—old wheat—wrapped around her head.

Harleigh Cemetery, Camden

Having posed, giddy tourists, in front of Whitman's grave, my friend leads me toward a cluster of interred relatives. He's only there to see one, a cousin whose gore he'd been made to clean after the body was taken away, suicide by gunshot.

Not all of the stories we pass down are heartening.

Ashore

On 31 December 1817, New Year's Eve, two of my ancestors debarked the ship April at the port of New Castle, Delaware. The river was frozen. They, after disease and quarantine and the burning of the fields of Magden by Napoleon's troops, stood, again, on land. However I might like to interpret their story, might like to say it could teach me about faith or fortitude, what I think about is the kiss they might have given each other, settling into sleep, first night in a new land.

WITNESS

Widowmaker

A friend's brother is in for surgery on his left anterior artery descending, and I think of heavy branches falling, men crushed by all the things they can't see.

Then, the Wye Oak, once the largest white oak in the country, standing since the 1500s. On one visit, I was fixed not on the tree itself, but the wires and suspensions arborists used to keep it together, and in that moment, such vast sadness—the heroic preservation of the tree looked painful and worked against its nature. It wasn't permitted to break apart, to make space and food and shelter for other trees, other critters, though it was casting off acorns.

When it came down in a storm in 2002, I was gutted. It wasn't in my home range, but I felt the loss. Still, things happened with the wood. A governor's desk, a sculpture, serving bowls. Paul Reed Smith Guitars got a little to make instruments, which somehow made it bearable, music coming out of this lost tree leading forward.

Again, I think of my friend's brother, the stenting, the propping-up of his heart and the good of having more time, more music to hear in his forward-life before he's wrecked by the final shattering storm.

Before the Inauguration

(January 2017)

I thought I could hedge the despair I felt with a visit to the National Arboretum and the original (1828) Virginia sandstone columns of the Capitol's East Portico. These columns stood as witness to Lincoln's two inaugurations and, at the second, to a parade in which African Americans marched, formally participating for the first time in inaugural events.

On that day, I didn't yet know the same bible on which Lincoln placed his hand would be used again, but I desperately wanted to believe in "the better angels of our nature," however absent they might have seemed in the flood of disheartening stories I was reading, daily, in the news.

I also did not know the Arboretum contains the National Bonsai and Penjing Museum, a collection started with a donation of Chinese penjing to Nixon, bolstered by the Nippon Bonsai Association's donation of 53 bonsai in celebration of the U.S. Bicentennial in 1976.

Verb

Although I have always thought of *bonsai* as a noun, it is also used as a verb to describe the act of maintaining, of planting and growing and tending, these trees. It takes place over generations. Children trained by their parents in the wiring of branches, the trimming of growth. Those children train their children.

I think, here, about family possessions and the nouns that have been passed down through my own family, how carelessly I lost a silver spoon that came from one grandparent, how easily the stem of another was snapped by cold ice cream. My own verb-tending of plants has resulted in deaths, my care turned to carelessness, withered stems in dry pots.

Weeping in the Chinese Pavilion

On the cold Saturday of my visit, the full collection of bonsai and penjing was tucked into the Chinese pavilion, a kind of cross-cultural story of protection from the elements, huddling together. I had come to see the columns, be restored by their connection to a history I idealized, but the bonsai—their incredible age—reminded me of other trees—witness trees from the Civil War, Liberty Trees from the Revolution. A startling number of these bonsai were time-witnesses to those same events.

I had not, until I was prompted by the placard, thought about WWII, Oppenheimer, or Hiroshima, where this bonsai was tended and where, by the happenstance of a well-placed wall, it survived atomic-shockwave destruction. Katie Nodjimbadem writes, "The bomb wiped out 90 percent of the city, killing 80,000 Japanese immediately and eventually contributing to the death of at least 100,000 more." Nodjimbadem describes the way by which Maseru Yamaki's bonsai came to be at the Arboretum, how his story was uncovered.

His story had to be uncovered; he didn't tell it.

The label identifies it as #2 of the original 53, "in training" since 1625. It was donated from Hiroshima. That word—*Hiroshima*—left me weeping in the
Chinese pavilion.

It was probably 1972 when Maseru Yamaki decided to gift this beauty his family had been bonsai-ing for six generations to the United States to celebrate its bicentennial. The educational film describes the members of the Nippon Bonsai Association preparing the plants to be crated to the U.S. as though the bonsai are daughters dressed for a wedding in another country.

This was only 27 years after *Little Boy.*

Viewfinder

Among the glass plates made by Alexander Gardner in late September 1862 is a stereograph: "Antietam, Maryland. Graves of Federal soldiers at Burnside Bridge." With a stereoscope, one could look at these paired images and see in three dimensions a man leaning as though at leisure, a stone fence, an edge of a bridge, a young sycamore, and finally, almost blending into the fence, the line-laid flat-stone markers of at least fourteen graves.

Snapshots

Stand at either end of the Burnside Bridge today, and watch visitor after visitor take photographs—of the bridge, of themselves on the bridge, the view up or down Antietam Creek. Its structure is graceful, arch after arch within arch on a form standard to the region, but visitors come here because it's marked by death, elevated by history.

Even Gardner, closer to that history, that death, took plate after plate there. On one, the negative sleeve marked "Burnside Bridge, across the Antietam, South-west view," the exposure delay captures the sweep of the current. It is just a lovely photograph of a lovely bridge, trees and mist in the air. There are no corpses awaiting burial, no blood in the water.

Witness

Gardner's repeated choice to photograph the Burnside Bridge documents the Burnside Sycamore a Witness Tree. There are surely other witnesses in the park, but they can't be so clearly known, merely aged by circumference at breast height.

The sycamore is known because Gardner witnessed it witnessing the aftermath, its peeling, whitened branches spectral over Antietam Creek.

To look at it now is a balm, its leafed crown dappling the bridge. One hardly notices the two eyebolts, the cables, the bark healing over the conservation hardware.

"Slips of yew silver'd in the moon's eclipse"

Not far from the Priest's Cave, on the grounds of Cong Abbey, are yews dating to about 1800, the ruins of the Abbey itself to the 13th C, though there was a church in the 7th C.

I read that yews are often planted in churchyards, and in that one line, I see so many bones, the urge to mark the dead with the living, bark-peeled branches giving shade and solace, and though I know the yew's a long-lived tree—easy symbol of immortality—I find myself thinking, instead, it was used to purify burial sites of plague victims, a different sort of superstition.

Carrying

The women in my family taught me how to sit with others' grief. My mother, her mother, the mothers back for generations, their quiet, gentle eyes.

On the drive to a funeral, I scribble a note for myself: "How much of learning to love someone is learning how to grieve them?" But the service—sitting in radiant stories—re-frames that question. We grieve all sorts of conditions, death not withstanding, but maybe learning how to love someone is also learning how to echo them into the wider world, even if one particularity is lost, surface riffles circling an invisible stone.

Is this what witness trees do? The planted bodies of the dead become a different thing in their work. Like the churchyard yews, they purify, remind us time is so much longer than ourselves, let us touch the smoothness under peeled bark and feel the skin of all our dead ones brought back to our longing hands, even if we never could have known them, even if they were never ours to begin with.

When the Burnside Sycamore eventually dies, undercut by the creek or smothered by soil compaction at its roots, six of its seedlings wait to replace it. I can't help but think of parents and children, of the ways in which my mother's voice is confused for mine, which is also confused for my son's.

Will or can that sycamore seedling become indistinguishable from its "parent"? Can the cloned sapling of the Wye Oak planted in its wrecked place ever be seen as something other than a shadow? Won't that take four hundred years?

There are echoes of one in the other. Why else do I feel a resonance when I hear a folk song about threatening the revenuers, though it's been nearly a century since Uncle Norm pulled his father from the flames of an exploding prohibition still?

Other Witnesses

Does it matter if the others are only "potential" witness trees at Antietam?

The park visitor sees the West and East Woods as being the trees through which the minie balls whizzed. We walk into these or other woods and presume the trees far older, even when we know about waves of deforestation.

Near my home is a grove of hemlocks at least 300 years old. Their battles are unsigned, uninterpreted, though they would have stood through loss of lands, of shifting borders, of the Massawomeck, the French, the British, so many feet springing over their fallen needles. Within the branches are no bracing cables, no wires, no metal plates, no concrete filling the rot.

In that silent, ancient-seeming place, I feel my own shifting hollows, witness my own losses laid bare in empty hands.

ACKNOWLEDGEMENTS AND APPRECIATIONS

An early draft of "Triage" was composed during the Allegany Arts Council's *Start to Finish* residency in January 2018. A version of "Drinking in Appalachia" was composed in 2016 for but not accepted to the *Looking at Appalachia Project.* Those generative opportunities forced my hand, and I'm grateful.

This book and I have been improved by Barbara Hurd, Stephen Dunn, Nina Forsythe, CJ Moll, Jim Ralston, Bryon MacWilliams, Patricia Henley, Jack DuBose, Mary Spalding-Kerns, Maggie Smith, Gerry LaFemina, Robert Hein, Indran Amirthanayagam, and John Burroughs. In such richness, I am indebted.

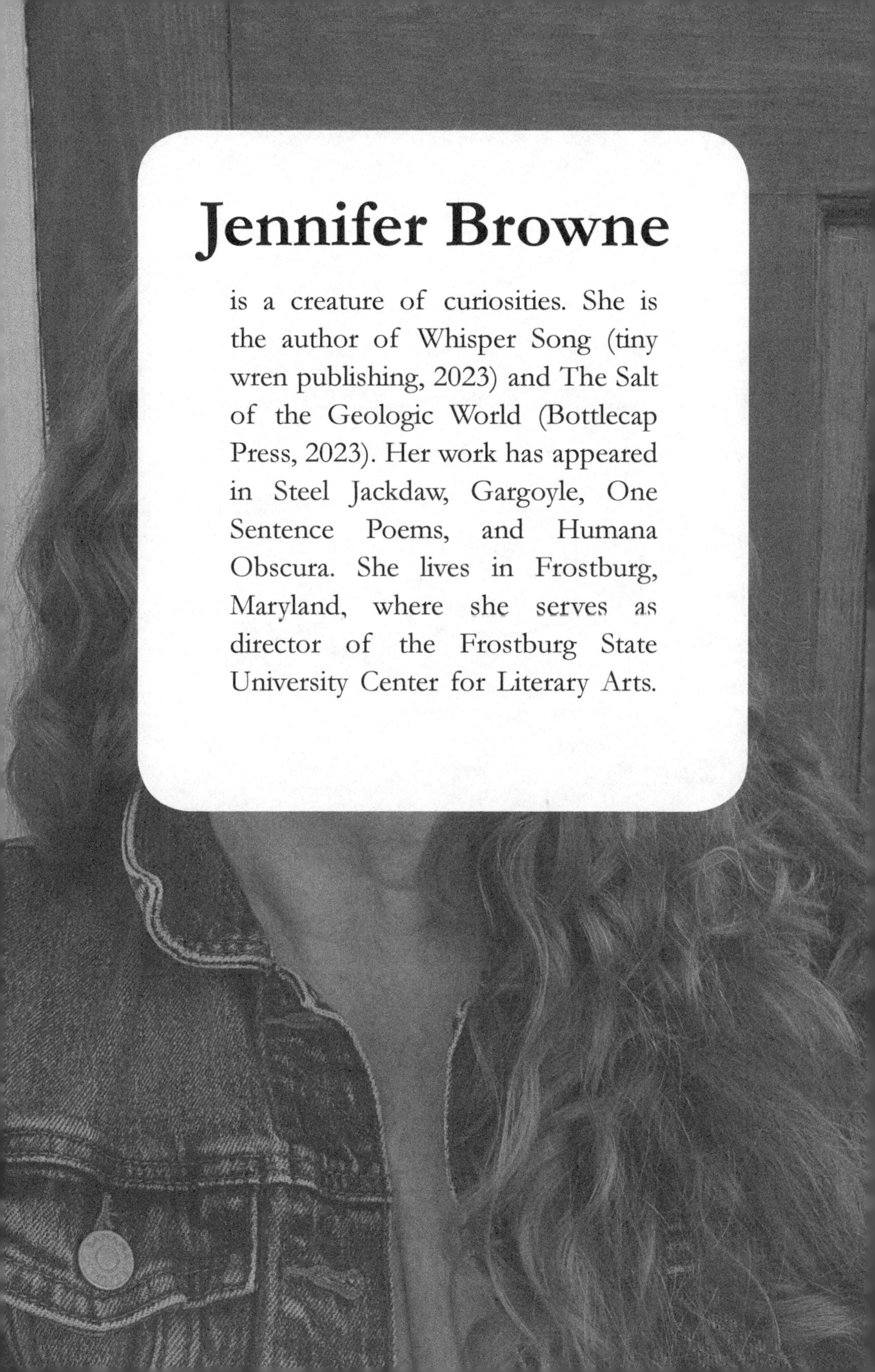

Jennifer Browne

is a creature of curiosities. She is the author of Whisper Song (tiny wren publishing, 2023) and The Salt of the Geologic World (Bottlecap Press, 2023). Her work has appeared in Steel Jackdaw, Gargoyle, One Sentence Poems, and Humana Obscura. She lives in Frostburg, Maryland, where she serves as director of the Frostburg State University Center for Literary Arts.

AMERICAN CROW

PRINTING WAS COMPLETED IN JULY 2024 FOR **Beltway Editions**